I0167676

JESUS, THE HUMAN AND THE BUTTERFLY

BY

KORRICKIA A. PETTY

LIFE TO LEGACY

Printed in the United States

10 9 8 7 6 5 4 3 2 1

Cover design by: Tasha Alexander, Legacy Design Inc
                  Legacydesigninc@gmail.com

Published by: Life To Legacy, LLC
15255 S. 94th Ave, 5th Floor
Orland Park, IL 60462
877-267-7477

Life2legacybooks@att.net

Table of Contents

Introduction

Upon this earth, we tend to exist in similar ways as the caterpillar. We are unaware of our true identity and potential. We crawl upon this earth lost, wandering and searching for life's meaning.

We enter into a day when we stumble, caught, and our trials and tribulations inevitably create for us a cocoon, and we become trapped in darkness. In that state of internal transformation, we realize how helpless we are, unable to save ourselves out of despair. The time has approached for the old creature to die because Jesus Christ died.

Suddenly, God's amazing grace through the Light of our Lord and Savior Jesus Christ, shatters the cocoon and penetrates our hard hearts. Our faith in Someone who can save us from the darkness of sin, save us from the entrapment of our circumstances becomes our Reality, our Truth. We surrender to a Love, Peace, Joy and Power beyond our own understanding. We become free and our true identity emerges—who God the Father created us to become is now manifested. His Love, His Words, His Life, His Shape, His Colors—being made into His Image and Likeness. We can now take flight into God's Presence and Purpose. The time has approached for the new creature to live, because Jesus Christ lives!

Our new lives begins with Jesus being the center of our inner existence, only from Him can our lives bring forth True Life & Fruit that can only be found in His Word.

Therefore, if any man be in Christ, he is a new creature. The old has passed away; behold the new has come. II Cor. 5:17

Chapter 1

GOD'S SOVEREIGNTY
HE DOES AS HE PLEASES

And God said, "Let us make man in our image, after our likeness: and let them have dominion over the fish of the sea, and over the fowl of the air, and over the cattle, and over all the earth, and over every creeping thing that creepeth upon the earth. So God created man in his own image, in the image of God created he him: male and female created he them. And God blessed them, and God said unto them, "Be fruitful and multiply, and replenish the earth, and subdue it: and have dominion over the fish of the sea, and over the fowl of the air, and over every living thing that moveth upon the earth (Genesis 1:26-28).

And the Lord God formed man of the dust of the ground, and breathed into his nostrils the breath of life, and man became a living soul (Genesis 2:7).

And the Lord God said, it is not good that the man should be alone; I will make him an help meet for him. Genesis 2:18

And the rib, which the Lord God had taken from man,

made he a woman, and brought her unto the man. And Adam said, This is now bone of my bones, and flesh of my flesh: she shall be called Woman, because she was taken out of Man. Therefore shall a man leave his father and his mother, and shall cleave unto his wife: and they shall be one flesh. And they were both naked, the man and his wife, and were not ashamed (Genesis 2:22-25).

To whom all praise, glory, honor and majesty is due! God Our Father, Lord Jesus Christ, the Son, and the precious Holy Spirit. You have spoken to all of creation from the beginning. Our Creator, who specifically and purposefully designed to the very last detail to how You wanted Your creation to exist and to function. You created the heavens and earth that You may have a foundation upon which to build. The light separated from the darkness that the distinction be made and each would know its purpose. You saw that it was good. The herb yielding seed, and the fruit-tree yielding fruit after its kind. The earth knew to bring forth grass. The waters brought forth abundantly, the whales, the fish after their kind, being fruitful and multiplying, and God saw that this was good. Every winged fowl and creeping things, the Lord saw that this was good. Man and woman created in His image. The image of perfection and holiness, spirit, mind, body and soul. And God saw that this was good. And God blessed the seventh day and sanctified it: because that in it he had rested from all his work which God created and made. Genesis 2:3. The Lord could rest now; everything is complete and perfect; to the finest detail. He is eternally glorified! Every part of creation now knows its purpose, and its function because the Almighty Creator God wouldn't have it no other way. His word was spoken and it was so!

You would think that the conscience of man would at least allow him to look into the depths of creation and see all God's wonderful handiwork. They should say "surely man couldn't have the ability to make all this creation; the clouds, rain and snow, the forest and the trees, the lightning and the sounds of thunder are evidence of Your awesome majesty. Consider all the fowls of the air, the fish of the sea, and beyond this green earth, the sun, moon, stars and galaxies, all give glory to God. Just as amazing as outer space are the miracles of inner space the place where babies are fashioned in secret, deep within the mother's womb. What about the mysteries of life where some people die young, and others live long productive lives. It's God who sets the boundaries of life that no man can surpass. Think about how fearfully and wonderfully made we are. No man-made machine or device can outperform our heart, lungs, liver, brain, cells, teeth, hands, feet our eyes or our blood. All of this splendiferous creation contained in our bodies, created in the image of God, are manifest evidence of God power and majesty. "Surely!" But Ecclesiastes 3:11 makes it very clear to us that the Lord has made everything beautiful in its time, He has also set eternity into man's heart, yet so he cannot find out what God has done from the beginning to the end. In Romans, the Apostle Paul makes a very compelling case where he writes,

> Because that which may be known of God is manifest in them; for God hath shewed it unto them. For the invisible things of him from the creation of the world are clearly seen, being understood by the things that are made, even his eternal power and Godhead, so they are

without excuse: Because that, when they knew God, they glorified him not as God, neither were thankful; but became vain in their imaginations, and their foolish heart was darkened.

Romans 1:19-21

Chapter 2
CATERPILLAR–OLD MAN

One of the first signs of a corrupt and defiled conscience is man's inability to grasp the fact is that we do not belong to ourselves. We have a Creator who chose to form us from the dust of the earth and breathed into us the breath of life. All that we are, or will ever become begins and ends with the Lord our Creator. If a soul continues to live in denial and the rejection of his Creator, well then he will find himself in a place of utter confusion, lostness, and hopelessness. Have we ever stopped to think about why we ask ourselves such questions as, "Who am I?" "Where do I come from?" "What am I supposed to be doing with my life?" The longing and desire to the answers and to the questions were placed there by our Creator. We are the finite created by the infinite, in all of our intellect, understanding, and developments in this present world. We are limited, dependent, and very needy upon the one true God who made us. Our hearts would not beat another beat, if the Lord didn't allow His breath to blow on us. We would starve if the Lord decided to dry up just a third of the water and earth that He so magnificently spoke into existence. So when we began to question and then seek for answers, where do we begin looking? What well do we draw from? Whose footsteps do we begin to walk in? Where do we go and to whom do we talk to? The questions began to pile up in our minds. So we began to wander from place to place and faces to faces in order to search out some definite meaning and worth to our existence. Asking ourselves, "What does this all mean?"

Interestingly to know is when we examine the life of the caterpillar, it's outward physical appearance will resemble the plant upon which it feeds. The insect can become camouflaged within its environment. Its identity is defined and shaped by that which it chooses to consume. If the plant is poisonous, then the insect becomes dangerous to its predators, and vice versa. It becomes just like the environment it inhabits. If its predators do not destroy the caterpillar, it will live to reach its full potential.

When we began to look to the external and feed on the things of this world, such as, money, materialism, status, positions, celebrities, and relationships to answer these questions we have pressuring our minds, instead of our Creator, then these things began to define who we are. The same fatal error Adam and Eve made from the beginning. They allowed the serpent, who was Satan to beguile and tempt their flesh with an external thing the Lord God forbade them to consume. So that very thing became a part of them and corrupted the entire nature of mankind, bringing forth sin and death. The pure and holy was cut off from them, they were forced to flee from the Garden of Eden. Man chose to consume that thing that poisoned him, which produced the fruit of sin, corruption and rebellion, causing the fall of man and all of creation. The Lord commanded

"...cursed is the ground for thy sake; in sorrow shalt thou eat of it all the days of thy life; Thorns and thistles shall it bring forth to thee; and thou shalt eat the herb of the field; In the sweat of thy face shalt thou eat bread, till thou return unto the ground; for out of it wast thou taken: for dust thou art, and unto dust shalt thou return.

Genesis 3:17-19

Man brought great sorrow and suffering upon himself and because he chose not to look to his Creator who formed him from the dust of the ground, defined him, gave him authority and dominion over all of His creation, what privilege was bestowed upon him.

Here we see the beginning of an identity crisis taking shape. The elephant wasn't created to teach the bird how to fly. The fish wouldn't dare try to walk on land as the mighty lion. I appreciate the trees giving me shade from the hot sun, instead of attempting to come into my lungs suppressing my ability to breathe the fresh air that the Lord God purposed for it do. So why would God's greatest creation, man, look to anyone or anything besides the one true God who created him. There is nothing but pure absurdity in this, yes, a form of insanity. This is what sin has done. When we choose to listen to what society and the world says we should be, we are misled every time.

We now have a government that has declared open rebellion to God, with its laws and decrees of abominations that are contrary to the word of God. The enemy told Eve, "that their eyes shall be opened, and ye shall be as gods, knowing good and evil." The serpent lied and deceived Eve into believing she could become something or someone God never intended for her to become. We are all familiar with this form of beguilement and deception that has plagued all of humanity. The serpent is continuing to lie to those who do not believe that marriage was created by Yahweh between a man and woman only. Those who believe in false religions such as Islam, Buddhism, Hinduism and New Age beliefs (that man can be his own god), are deceived. Many beliefs that Roman Catholicism hold are contrary to sound biblical, doctrinal beliefs, are being led astray and deceived by the enemy of their souls, but there is hope. Many will be saved and delivered from this kind of deception. Jesus is the way, the truth and the life, no man cometh unto the Father but by Me, John 14:6.

Chapter 3
FORMED IN THE WOMB

As a young girl, during my elementary years I remember a childhood of fun, curiosity and discovery. I was very smart in school and made friends easily. I grew up in a big family, so I had aunts, uncles and cousins and of course my grandma to help raise me. I don't ever remember being without all the necessities of life and having my needs met. I can't explain though as a child why I began early having sexual perversion issues. There were times I would have sexual experiences with my female cousins usually by touching and kissing. Other times there would be sexual encounters with the neighborhood boys. Were these normal experiences that children go through? Why was I having these feelings? We had to hide, and you better not say anything. Growing up I struggled with my sexual identity. I never felt like there was anyone in my family at the time that I could turn to, or who could help me understand these feelings I were experiencing at that time of my childhood. There were times I felt very alone as a child, even though I grew up within a large, extended family. As I reflect back, I started to feel isolated and rejected. I remember these feelings of rejection began to take even greater effects upon me, when my mother would leave and go out on dates with my brother's father at that time. My feelings would be very hurt because I didn't know when she would leave or when she would come back. Again the feelings of rejection would eventually have more devastating effects during my teenage years on into adulthood.

One of the most fondest memories I had with my mother, was when she would hold me in her lap. I would place the frame of my little face in the cup of her neck, allowing the scent of her Halston perfume be a refreshing comfort of her love and tenderness towards me. I understand now my mother could not give me no more or no less than what she had on the inside of her.

I attended vacation bible school one summer, school was out and I was having the time of my life just like any other child my age. I believe I was 11 or 12, kinda hard to remember. Two things stands out for me during that experience. I heard about Jesus and I remember my mother taking me to church as a young child. I would fall asleep then be painfully awakened by my mother's hard pinches, only to wake up mad or crying, then dosing right back off again. Looking back now, pain is usually what the Lord will use to wake us up to the hearing of the gospel and His word. So, I heard the gospel. For God so loved the world, that He gave His only begotten Son, that whosoever believeth in Him, shall not perish, but have everlasting life. John 3:16. This verse of scripture is the one I'd learned and the one verse that the Lord would bring back to my remembrance(explain more later). I was baptized during the vacation bible school. Secondly, I remember us having a program towards the end. I was allowed to lead a song, but during that song, I felt something different, then I began to cry and weep, but I kept on trying to sing. Then as the days of my young life went on I remember there were times when I would try to read the Bible, but never having an understanding or clue to what I was reading. So, growing up I always believed in the Lord, and there were times I would continue to pray and read the Bible. But still nothing. During my teenage years, I didn't attend church much at all. I grew up in a home where church and God weren't discussed much, and definitely not much Bible reading. I did not know the Lord, nor did I have a relationship with Him. But I believed without a doubt; a seed was planted within me during vacation bible school, not understanding until now, that later on God would bring the increase.

My childhood was typically like any other little black girl growing up in the south. So much fun, riding bikes, freeze cups, going to parks and growing up with many cousins and friends. Burnt bologna sandwiches to buy-one-get-one-free Big Mac coupons. Jungle juice, cupcakes and 'tater chips..my favorites. Even some neighborhood fights and knee scraps helped shape and mold me. I come from a large family, so there was always family around to help raise and take care of me. My mother was a teenager, fifteen years old when she became pregnant with me. She and my biological father, well you know the story, didn't make it. I remember him last coming around during my elementary years, but unfortunately, we weren't able to bond, so I grew up without him. My mother would later become pregnant again with my brother and marry his father. When I was around twelve or thirteen, we all moved from my grandmother's to a very small house in south Memphis. I did not like it at all. Interestingly to know is this was around the same time I was baptized in vacation bible summer school and my childhood began to change drastically. "She just acting like a b-t-h." When I first heard this word spoken about me, I was devastated. My feelings were very hurt and I didn't know how to deal with this kind of language spoken about me.

What made it even worse, was that my mother did not take up for me. To this day, I can't remember what I did to deserve being called such as name, but that part I can't forget, as with so many other memories. From that day on, would come ongoing mental, emotional and verbal abuse. I grew up in a home as with so many young black children during that age, coming up in the 80's. Where if you had anything, the "dope game" as many would call it, was the only way you were going to eat. I remember the parties, seeing cocaine powder covering the table and weed smoke filling the rooms. Flashing cash around like it what'n nothing. "How much you want?" Coach bags, Louis Vuitton and all the clothes you wanted boosted hot off the racks from Dillard's, Goldsmith's and who knows where else. I knew a lot of things just weren't right, but who was I, just a child, not realizing how much danger my life was in at the time.

Not only my life but all of our lives. We were caught up in all of the material gain and people in the neighborhood thinking we were something. But I know many people knew in the neighborhood and it actually became an embarrassment to me about how my family made money. My stepfather and I did not have a good relationship at all while I was growing up. He would provide us with the necessities of life and like I stated earlier, many materialistic things. He was emotionally and verbally abusive towards me. One of the worst incidences I can remember is when we were at "the diner," we had a restaurant also. Me, my mother, and brother would work there on the weekends to help. Lord have mercy, it was hard and tiring. One weekend my brother and I got into it about something. Then my response about what happened wasn't received so well. My stepfather told me to come to the back office. He took his fist and knocked me over my head, and as I fell back onto the couch, he then took a pistol out of his pocket as to threaten me some more. Again, my mother, defenseless, passive and afraid. She did not come to my rescue. This cycle would continue on and on into my teenage and pre-adult years. I hated my stepfather so much. So many days I wished he was dead. So many days I wanted to run away. I felt nothing but hatred from him and towards him. I was afraid of him, not knowing what he may ever do to me. I believe no one really cared or could help me, because those on the outside were blinded by the lifestyle they saw us living. My stepfather could put on a good show in front of others by the flash and cash, and being nice to strangers and giving others much material gain, but behind closed doors, he was a monster. The yelling, cursing and anger constantly, day in day out. Of course, my mother and I was not as close as we should have been. There was so much control and fear within the relationship with my stepfather that I believe even if she ever said or done anything, she would pay the repercussions one way or another. As the time was approaching for me to graduate from high school, I was so happy.

Chapter 4
ILLUSIONAL WAY OF ESCAPE

My dream of becoming a nurse was just beginning. My first year of college was so much fun and discovery...too much fun. I neglected to do right with my studies and ended up failing my first year. I was so pitiful. Again, struggling with my sexual identity, this would be the time, I would have my first and last lesbian experience. It was nothing like I thought it would be, and actually, I just did not like it. I felt really ashamed afterward. I wrote a letter to the young lady and asked her to please not tell anyone. But to this day, I don't know for sure if she ever told anyone. I had to go back home to the hell I was hoping I'd escaped.

That summer I began drinking and smoking weed much heavier, trying to cope with everything I was facing and trying to stay in school and clean up my mess. Things got really intense again nearing the end of the summer at home. Next thing I know, I was kicked out, at my grandmother's, and Jack shows up at the door with all of my belongings thrown up in my blanket. Dude just said, "here ya stuff Billie," that was another nickname they called me. Again, I was broken and felt like crap. But I continued going to school and fought my way beyond all the discouragement and pain. I refused to give up. I later returned to my mother's home, and I would just try to stay out of the way, and ride the city bus to the local community college to get myself back on track with school.

During college, I was finally focused and determined to work hard and finish what I had started. My dream of becoming a nurse was coming to pass. I had to study long and hard to accomplish my goal. It was not that easy for me.

It was the summer of 1997, a year before my graduation from college when I met Ken. We immediately connected because of all the weed we enjoyed smoking together. It was truly by the grace of God I'd made it this far. I would say he was the first serious boyfriend I ever had. I had one of the best times of my life. Ken gave me the attention I was longing for and he was just simply really kind to me. We would have the all-night long conversations, and I begin to spend most of my time with him. We started out like most couples, infatuated, sharing our hopes, dreams and imagining what our futures would consist of.

I wasn't all the attracted to him at first. I was just trying to have the time of my life before graduation and on into the world of major responsibilities. I was so green. Ken and I started talking more and more, becoming closer. He was able to come to my graduation and from there on, our story progressed. I graduated May 1998, and got my first nursing job. I was so happy. What an amazing accomplishment, realizing a dream coming true.

In August of that same year, I found out I was pregnant. I wasn't that surprised because I was not protecting myself every time we engaged in premarital sex (sin is only pleasurable for a season).

I definitely wasn't ready for this. I thought about an abortion, but was too afraid to do it.

After I told Ken, he seemed to be happy about it—a little too happy. I started to wonder in my stupidity, "did he do this on purpose," as if he did it alone, without my consent and help. Ken didn't seem to be worried about it at all, he appeared to be excited about the pregnancy. "Did he plan this?" "A set-up?" It takes two right! After we'd accepted the fact that we were about to become parents, we soon made the decision to get an apartment together and try to make something work.

Ken had such a creative mind and a gift with words. It was one of the reasons I fell in love with him. He would write letters that really made me feel he loved and cared about me. Not realizing this at the time, of course, most of us start out in relationships eating the cake before finding out the ingredients. Ken and I loved each other to the best we knew how, but later only to learn, that without the love of God dwelling richly in our hearts we will never come to knowing how to really love unconditionally the way the Lord intended for us to love.

I finally told my Mom. The first thing she said was, "how is he going to take care of y'all?" But what I say, "all Ma, we'll be fine, I'm working, he works.

Chapter 5
COCOON—TRANSFORM

The butterfly cocoon is such an interesting process that the caterpillar initiates by spinning this silky, glue-like substance around its body as a protective casing. Once the casing is formed, the caterpillar then begins this process of digesting itself to some type of liquid being held within the cocoon. Then what remains are these discs that eventually mature into the body of the you know what (we will get there a little later). The caterpillar actually dies.

> Verily verily, I say unto you, Except a corn of wheat fall into the ground and die, it abideth alone: but if it die, it bringeth forth much fruit.
>
> John 12:24

My life would progress on into adulthood where the externals would define who I was. Now understand, I am in no way condemning education, achievements, financial and material successes, but they are nothing but dung, as the Holy Spirit led Paul to put it if we are without Christ Jesus. That's where I found myself, lost in a world of materialism, greed and self-seeking pleasures of this life. I was able to make it through nursing school and was able to work really hard to achieve the life the world said would make you somebody, and you can have this and that and go here and there. I had opportunity after opportunity to earn money as long as I was physically able to endure it. There seemed like it was no end to the madness, and I enjoyed it. I was satisfied and content. I felt like I could do whatever I wanted to do. I gladly accepted the title as a work-aholic, I didn't care, but I wasn't broke and didn't have to ask anyone for anything, oh I wouldn't dare. That was my attitude. I had planned my entire life, career, marriage, job; you name it. I had to be in control of every aspect. But how many of us realize now that everything will not go as you plan it. It is only by God's amazing, undeserving grace towards us that He would allow some of the things to take place in our lives that we ask for, how awesome He is.

Things seemed to have been working out for us. I was working as much I wanted to, Ken worked and we were able to afford the things we needed. We never had trouble paying our bills and from the outside looking in, you would think we were doing just fine. I was earning up to a six-figure salary at one point. We could take family trips and do so many things, us and our kids not wanting for nothing, but internal chaos and torment was beginning to set in and manifest in unimaginable ways. The very life we choose to live outside of the will God began to consume and destroy us in ways we could have never fathom. We made this bed; now we are going to have to lay in it. The consequences of doing things our way and not God's way brought much pain and suffering. The caterpillar can only digest that which it is familiar. When the mind and spirit of a man are darkened, he or she will choose darkness.

"And this is the condemnation that light is come into the world, and men loved darkness rather than light, because their deeds were evil" (John 3:19).

Chapter 6
KEEP TRANSFORMING

Our daughter is born. The most beautiful and precious gift I could ever receive. I was so happy to be a mother, absolutely no regrets. My baby girl entered into this world with her own little struggles. I had to leave her in the ICU and go home without her. This was not good at all for me. I delivered Kymmia early, she was premature and needed to become more stable in her condition. After my delivery with my baby girl, I took a turn for the worse and developed what is called pulmonary edema, excessive fluid build-up in the lungs. It became very difficult for me to breath. Thank the Lord for the quick responses of my caregivers and the much-needed oxygen and medications that were available; I was able to pull through. Ken and I experienced what most barely-know-what-we-are-doing folks with a new baby does. We were both so happy to have her and loved our baby, giving her all the attention and care she deserved.

In between working, keeping the bills paid, diapers, pick-ups, drop-offs; it all definitely became overwhelming a lot of days. We didn't realize it at the time, but the consequences of the choices we made were starting to manifest. The time of reaping what we had been sowing has come. As time went on, I noticed how the mounting responsibilities and cares of life started to bring on more stress and discord between us. The communication began to dwindle and time spent with one another began to lesson. More time being spent with others instead of each other started to take its toll...distance. The arguments and fights and other women and men, silent treatments, verbal and emotional abuse, control battles...when does it all end. Oh everybody goes through this right, it's alright, y'all will make, y'all got that baby, y'all need to try and work things out.

"I don't feel good. What's wrong? I didn't get the job. Why not, what happened?" I failed the physical, they said my blood pressure and blood sugar was too high. When I met Ken, he had already been diagnosed with diabetes as a teenager. He had been struggling and having a difficult time managing it at times, so I would help him as much as I could and knew how. I believed he appreciated my help most of the time, but I learned also a person going through what he was experiencing can also become resentful towards those wanting to help them. Illness can take its toll on anyone and impacts the entire family. Ken and I would have many arguments about his unwillingness to take better care of himself and the mounting fears I began to have about if something were to ever happen to him.

"Hello, you don't know me, my name is S. I just want you to know Ken and I are together, and I just had twins, and they are his. Can we meet?" "Okay, no I don't want to meet you," I told her. As I was taking a bath and Kymmia, just barely a year old, standing beside the tub is when I received this devastation. What do I do, is she telling the truth? Ken admitted to knowing this woman and that they had been sexually involved, but the babies were not his. The dying begins. Our relationship began to suffer like never before. What trust? Now we have this baby. I never wanted to be a single mother and definitely was not going to stand for another man raising my child. I no longer wanted the relationship, but at the same time I felt like I couldn't leave. Then one day Ken came to me and said that he was going back to Mississippi, that's when I decided to give him another chance. I did not want him doing that. I started to feel like many of the problems we were having was because we were not married and doing things the right way. So we began discussing the need for marriage since we both had decided then that we both weren't going anywhere.

Ken proposed, and then we went shopping for rings and found a his and hers set for about eight-hundred and some dollars. We had decided that we didn't want anything big and fancy, and definitely keep it within our budget. We found us something nice to wear and got married at my folks house. Ken's family from Starkville came down, my friends and family of course, and we had a beautiful time. My cousin Carla fixed us a beautiful cake and the food was fantastic. Our precious Kymmia was two years old at the time and able to run around and celebrate with us. I was so happy we did the right thing to commit to each for the rest of our lives. After the wedding, we were able to spend our honeymoon in Jamaica. What an experience! We had the opportunity to travel up the mountainous countryside and really take on some sites most tourist may not typically see. We actually climbed a steep mountain and went into a cave. The first time we ate a sweet, juicy mango. It was so hot, my sweat was sweating, but we made it and went on to have a really nice time.

It was April 28, 2001 our wedding day and weeks later, I found out I was pregnant. My time of carrying my son was a joyous one. Thank the Lord, I didn't allow myself to go through some of the things I'd experienced carrying Kymmia, learning from previous choices. It wasn't until after my delivery is when I went through the same thing I suffered with my daughter's delivery, but this time it was me having to spend a couple of days in the intensive care unit. Soon after Kj was born and I had the chance to hold him for the first time, one of the most amazing experiences a mother can have. I suddenly became short of breath and had difficulty with a rapidly beating heart rate. The nurses quickly had to prepare me for transfer to the ICU. When I woke up, I could see my family members at my bedside. The cardiologist told me that I had gone into congestive heart failure. This diagnoses I refused to accept without a fight. So grateful for the knowledge and training I had as a nurse, I was able to question and try to put the pieces of the puzzle together. I didn't realize how sick I had gotten until later when I was able to speak with my caregivers. I finally recovered and my son and I was able to leave the hospital. Ken was a good father to our children. He loved spending time with them and was just always there for our children. I really didn't have many issues with him concerning them. Ken and our children were very close and I appreciated that as a mother.

We went on about our daily lives like most people, paying bills, raising a family and simply trying to make ends meet. Ken worked for a local youth facility for troubled children and eventually, he started to become tired of that kind of work. In 2004, he'd completed seven years of service, and just enough to receive a pension. "I'm tired of working!" "Say what!", I thought he'd just cussed me out. "No, you just need something else to do," I responded. After much arguing and attempting to figure out what would be the best decision, Ken eventually decided to take his pension, and the plan was to pay for barbering school. This was late spring, early summer when Ken would leave his job and things quickly began to spiral downward for us.

Chapter 7
FEARFUL REALITY

"I'm tired, I ain't been feeling good," Ken told me. "Well, you need to go on to the doctor." By October of that year, Ken saw the doctor and was diagnosed with end-stage renal disease. He would need dialysis for the rest of his life, unless he received a kidney transplant. My fears have now become a reality. Ken seemingly was taking the news as best he could. My years as a dialysis nurse, the warnings, the stories and the tears could not stop this from happening. But on the other hand my experience and knowledge gained in this area of practice, helped us both transition into this new and major change in our lives.

"You alright?" On our first visit to the nephrologist, we got into a bad accident. Thank God no one was seriously injured, including the drunk man that turned off in front of us. We weren't far from the doctor's office, so out of anger, Ken started walking. We finally sat down with Dr. Phillips and she proceeded to share with us all that we would have to do and face. Ken would later officially began his dialysis treatments that following year, January 2005. My fears and worries about Ken's health would finally come to pass. So as we prepared for this new journey, so many challenges would began to bombard us.

After I saw that Ken was tolerating and handling the dialysis treatments fairly well, it would give me much relief and assurance that we were going to be alright. Taking on the full financial responsibilities of the household started to take its toll. But poor money management, debt, and not making the necessary spending adjustments when Ken was no longer able to work became even a greater problem. So I found myself working more and more out of fear, worry, and just needing to get away from an increasingly depressing home environment. Since Ken was no longer working, majority of the responsibilities for our children fell on him. And at the time, my attitude was such as that. He should have taken on more in the home, since I had to continue working and paying all the bills. Not realizing that he also needed rest breaks due to the dialysis treatments. I believe he also struggled badly with not being able to contribute financially to our household like he would have liked. Even though, I would try my very best not to put any added pressure on him because of it. So much pressure, unbearable pressure would eventually lead us further and further apart.

The silence, the distance. Very little communication and eventually sleeping in separate beds. It's so disheartening that two people can love each other and have children, then eventually become strangers towards one another. Absent of love, affection and communication, the very things marriages and relationships are built upon. We don't realize it at the time, but when we choose to go our own way, instead of God's ordained and perfect plan for relationships and marriage, we will suffer extreme consequences.

And He answered and said unto them, Have ye not read, that He which made them at the beginning made them male and female. And said for this cause shall a man leave father and mother, and shall cleave to his wife: and they twain shall be one flesh? Wherefore they are no more twain, but one flesh. What therefore God has joined together, let not man put asunder.

Matthew 19:4-6

March of 2005, Ken's mother would pass after being a dialysis patient for several years, then complications from a failed kidney transplant. More pressure, then bouts of depression with both of us. Smoking weed and drinking and pills became my vices in order to cope with so many burdens. Ken continued smoking weed also, but these things were only making matters worse. We would eventually go on to separate for the first time that summer. After about two months, he came back home to us. Ken's disability income had begun by then, so that definitely helped us out more. Through many of the various changes Ken and I were facing, our children seemingly were coping alright.

The following year of 2006 looked liked we were going to make it through. We took our first trip to Disney Land in Florida. We had arranged Ken's dialysis treatments, everything was taken care of and we were so happy. We went through the parks, rode the rides and ate everything we could. So, so much fun. Ken had taken a part-time teaching job at our son's school. It was so good to see him moving on with his life, in spite of. Heading towards the fall of that year, I had to have gallbladder surgery, and needed time off work. Of course, there were again financial concerns, and the bills being taken care. Up until this time, we rarely had issues about putting our money together as a family to make sure things were taken care of. "I'm going to need to keep my check." "You what!" Ken had decided that he no longer wanted to help out on the bills anymore. I didn't understand. I was so angry and hurt. "What's going on, what are you doing with your money then?" "You got to do something!" Days later, as I was lying in the bed. It was September of that year. Ken woke me up and ask me for ten dollars for gas money. I couldn't believe it. "You just got your check!" "Please what's wrong, what's going on Ken?" How come you don't have any money. I then started to question, could it be the weed? Was he spending too much money on weed?" Could it be someone he was seeing? Later on to find out, that he was playing cards and gambling. Staying gone some days, all night. I was beyond tired. I cannot take this anymore. I felt like I was taking on enough weight. Now the income that he was getting every month, he wanted to take it away, and continue asking me for money. After Ken had told me that he couldn't help pay bills anymore, I told him he couldn't ask me for anything or get nothing from me. Furious!

Chapter 8
COCOON DEATH CONTINUES

"Where are you going?" I'm bout to go out. I no longer cared about my marriage, or being there anymore. I no longer respected Ken and did not want to be there. I was done with all of it. One night I had gone out clubbing, drinking and smoking more weed. I met this young man named Marvin. Marvin was slick like the rest of them. Fast-talking "ooh baby you so sexy, what's yo number?" "Come here girl." Yep, I fell for it. We exchanged numbers, and you know the rest becomes an awful history. Marvin would call me the following night and I decided to visit him at his apartment. We ended up having sex. "Damn, what's that smell?" I thought to myself. He had an odor coming from his penis, because he wasn't circumcised as a baby, and would hold more bacteria and cause odor. It was repulsive, but not even that stopped me. I just ignored it and continued in this madness. "Are you seeing somebody?" Ken asked. "Naw, I don't know what you mean. "Why are you asking me that?" Mane, I ain't no fool, I can just tell, "Mane I just got this feeling."

Days later I contacted a lawyer and filed for divorce. Ken kept saying he didn't want the divorce. But it was no way I was

KORRICKIA A. PETTY

staying; my mind was made up. The divorce process would go on from 2007 to spring 2009. This was one of the worse experiences I would ever face. The paperwork was endless, not to mention the legal fees. Ken couldn't afford a lawyer, but this older lady, who was very well-known in the city, decided to take his case. The nightmare ensued. The strongest argument his attorney could use against me was the fact that he was disabled, on dialysis, and could no longer work. They would later try to prove that it was abandonment and irreconcilable differences. The fact that I earned more money and was the "breadwinner," bolstered his defense. It was like sharks smelling blood in the water.

Ken's lawyer was both vicious and relentless; she left no stone unturned. It was so unnecessary because I was not seeking child support or anything else from Ken. However, that did not matter and weighed absolutely nothing. I just wanted him to be out of my life. I just wanted to be done. When it's over, it's over! So I thought. This was not going to end as quickly as I'd hoped it would. Again, this would turn out to be the worst thing I'd ever gone through at this point in my life. My life was spiraling out of control so badly, until I started seeing a man, who I would learn later was a warlock for the kingdom of darkness.

At that time I was just looking for answers from anyone I thought could help me fix my situation. This man would have me come into this small, back room and would sit me down at a table with him. He would then remove these beads and stones from a bag then throw them on the table in front of me. He would then begin to tell me personal things about my life, so I began to trust who and what he was doing for

-34-

me. I would pay him forty dollars every time I went to see him for about two months. I started to become a little afraid to continue dealing with him, once he began asking me about doing a sacrifice ritual with chickens. The last day I would see this man at his shop, was when this tall, light-skinned, slender man walked into the shop and greeted me. He was wearing all black, with straight black, permed hair, and he had pointed fingernails. Then when I looked at his hand, I could see a ring on his finger with a star in the center. I never went back. Later on after my deliverance, and the Lord Jesus pulled me from a horrible pit of hell, I would then turn on my television to watch the ministry broadcast of a very well-known preacher in the city. As the camera was zooming in on the choir, Lord have mercy, I see the warlock singing in the choir at this church.

Ken's lawyer would eventually argue that he needed money for gas and food when the kids would come over to visit him on the weekends. Setting up and even stronger foundation to gain child support and alimony. So during the divorce process, I was ordered to pay him $250.00 a month. More devastation. I continued working more and more overtime, trying to keep up the bills and expenses. All along I'd even gotten so bold as to move Marvin in with me and my kids. I didn't care. I would give him money to help him buy a car. He was broke too and eventually would turn out to be a whore. (Yeah, you right, who was I to talk), I will leave it right here about Marvin. Iron-ically, as I write (five years after my rebirth), the Lord would move my kids and I into a place less than five minutes around the corner from Marvin's apartment where I spent many days and nights on my way to hell. (BUT GOD!!!) So as I routinely drive by there, I can't help but be ever so grateful for how Jesus showed so much mercy and grace upon my soul. Sometimes I wonder if that's one of the reasons the Lord allowed me even to be so close to the pit He delivered me from, to remind me of His amazing love and grace He showed towards me.

My lawyer basically robbed me. It seemed like all I was doing was giving him my money and paperwork, money and paperwork, money and paperwork. Absolutely no results. I even went so far to spend a little over a thousand dollars for a private detective, because Ken was living with some female in an apartment for a while. So what was I to believe? When I gave my lawyer the videotape to present to the judge, this man came up with every excuse in the book not to use it. He claimed when he viewed it; he could not really see anything. I thought he was one of the worst people in the world. I literally started to believe I am paying this man, and he is deliberately working against me. The case is between the lawyers for their benefit so that they can get paid. Whatever happens with the clients, oh well that's their business...get what they can get. All I knew was I was the losing big time. My life was spiraling down quickly. I begin having high blood pressure problems, and angry all of the time. I was very disrespectful to people, cursing folks out for no reason. One morning I'd stop to get gas on my to work. As I was standing there pumping gas, a little old black lady seemingly appeared from nowhere and handed me a small piece of folded paper with some words about God written on it. I took it and just continued pumping, not thinking much about it. Then as I look back on that day, I don't remember seeing where she had gone that quickly. I was so miserable at work, and began to hate going. I was coming home drinking two bottles of merlot and taking 75 mg of Tylenol p.m. and sleeping pills, when I wasn't smoking. My family knew it was bad, but they didn't know to the extreme of what was happening to me. I felt like I was buried in nine feet of dirt up to my neck. The last foot of dirt that would come to cover my head and bury me was after two years, and some weeks of going through the divorce proceedings, I received a petition from Ken's lawyer stating that he wanted full custody of our kids due to infidelity. I thought no way was I going to be able to go through this any longer. The last thing they were going to do was take my children from me.

Towards the end of February, going into March of 2009, I found myself at home alone. My children were visiting their father at the time. I found myself in a horrible place of emptiness and darkness within my soul I can hardly describe. As I sat on my bed, I began to have thoughts of how I was going to murder my husband. The enemy had me plotting how to do it, and how I was going to get off. I saw myself walking into the dialysis clinic, and cutting the bloodlines, or just shooting him while he was on the dialysis machine. I even saw myself in an orange jumpsuit after my arrest. I was empty on the inside. I knew my body was there, but it didn't feel like I was there on the inside. As if my soul had left my body, and I felt like I was dead on the inside. I thought I was physically about to leave this world. This is the best way I can describe this experience.

Chapter 9

THE BUTTERFLY

Therefore, if any man be in Christ, he is a new creature, old things have passed, behold all things have become new.
2 Corinthians 5:17

Once the caterpillar has finally surrendered and her demise becomes imminent and is no more, the adult butterfly is now able to take shape. As form and growth begins to develop, a new body merges, wings are needing room to stretch forth to prepare to take flight. The enclosure becomes unbearable. Internal desperation forced a new identity to come forth. Darkness was no longer a place of comfort for the new creature. The shedding of the cocoon has allowed light to shine forth, bringing life, renewal, restoration and resurrection. A new identity, never to be the same ever again.

I began to call out to God and ask Him to take my mind. I just wanted something to be done with my mind. I couldn't say anything else. But Lord, please take my mind. Strangely, to this day, I don't remember even going to sleep that night. But when I woke up the next morning, I felt so much peace, love, and joy. I was so happy. I was running and jumping around the house. I felt light , the heaviness was gone, the pain was gone, the hurt was gone, the tears were gone. My mind was clear, my vision was clear. At the time though not fully comprehending what had just happened to me! All I knew was, I was just happy and felt great. The Lord reminded me of His voice that I'd heard,

John 3:16, "For God so loved the world, that He gave His only begotten Son, that whosoever believeth on Him shall not perish, but have everlasting life." My life would absolutely never, ever be the same. Thank You Lord Jesus! I understood now fully and completely what Jesus did for me on the cross. All the pain, hurt and suffering I was going through, Jesus suffered greatly for it all. That's what His death was for and about. He took all the pain, hurt, my sins, disappointments;all of it upon himself. Jesus did not stay dead, but He was raised forever more! And because He lives, I was able to live with Him, and be free from all that I was facing in my life at the time. It was a miracle! I truly felt like I had been born again, and I was! I was a totally different person.

Everything changes. My entire view of life was completely and totally different. I only wanted to know what God had to say about everything according to His word. His love is indescribable. Oh His Love! A love one can never know unless God shed it abroad in your heart by the Holy Spirit. (Romans 5). Glory! The peace of God is indescribable! I mean nothing could disturb me. Things began to change so beautifully for me. Father started drawing me to read His word more and more every day. That's all I wanted to do, and get to somebody's church as often as I could. I mean I thought I could get that word in me as quick as I could, I found myself in desperation to get it all in, until one night the Lord spoke to my heart to remind me that His word is eternal. It's not going anywhere, so it was alright to slow down and not become overly anxious I chuckle now as I write, and just think God is so Wonderful and Amazing and Awesome and Loving, Kind and Glorious forever and ever! The case and work would no longer take its toll on me. One day I was getting coffee and made a phone call to the lawyer to find out about the petition for custody of my children. The lawyer went on to say, "what petition?" "No petition for custody was found in the docket"! I ran into the bathroom, and hollered, screamed and cried! Just thanking and praising God! Lord have mercy I was so grateful and relieved. God was showing me then how He was going to fight this battle. Father placed me in such an amazing rest and peace with everything and everybody. All I wanted to do was talk about Jesus and tell people what happened to me. I remember writing my folks a long letter trying to explain it all to them. But of course, I got no response.

Most people would rather think you have gone crazy and lost your mind, then to be able to handle the fact that the Lord Jesus Christ came and saved my life! Hallelujah! I would later go on to serve in my local church as a Sunday school teacher. All the while trying to understand about gifts and callings. All I know, I would have dreams and visions. I would hear Scripture verses being spoken by this soft sweet voice in my sleep. Lord what is happening to me? Then all of a sudden I began to meet people, like the little old man, whose wife I was taking care of at work. I will never forget how he looked at me in my eyes. We just talked about God and the His word. I would read all day at work. I had to have my Bible at all times. The next day he brought me a book by Max Lucado, called John 3:16, with a beautiful inscription in it to encourage me in my walk with the Lord. Then the Lord would send person after person to confirm His word and call upon my life. These worldly things no longer mattered. I was not going to allow anything to keep me from the love and peace of God.

As time went on, I began to feel the need and conviction to separate from old friends and acquaintances. I was no longer comfortable hanging around them because I was no longer interested in doing the same things they were doing. At times when I would even attempt to go around here and there, I would feel the conviction. Until I finally had to accept and understand that the old me was dead now. Ephesians 2:1 And you hath He quickened, who were dead in trespasses and sins. Ephesians 2:5 Even when we were dead in sins, hath quickened us together with Christ, (by grace ye are saved)! I am a new creature in Christ. The Lord started working on my heart about Ken again, I felt so much love and peace within. I received the miracle of forgiveness. I had forgiven Ken, my family, and everyone who had ever hurt me. Father had brought such powerful healing and deliverance.

Chapter 10
RECONCILED WARFARE

I wanted my marriage back, so Ken and I started talking again. I believe Ken was tired also. So we stopped everything and reunited once more. So 2010 became another indescribable year of major changes we would face again. I would experience spiritual warfare on a level to where at one point, I would not make it out alive. Of course, it was difficult and hard for Ken to accept how my life and total existence had changed. I wanted to watch sermons and listen to gospel music all of the time. He didn't. I was in the habit of sleeping with my Bible every night. He had a problem with that. I wanted to go to church. He did start going to church with me, then he eventually stopped. He said I was just doing too much for him. In my efforts of trying to draw him, it seemed as if I was pushing him further and further away. He wanted to continue smoking weed in the house, and I could no longer stand to smell it and did not want even to see it. Glory be to God, I no longer had a desire for it.

After so much conflict, I began to question if I'd made another big mistake by us coming back together. Ken would eventually move into the other bedroom. We began to live that married-but-separated in the same house madness. Lord have mercy! No more intimacy, only time communication was longer than 30 minutes, was because we were arguing. It again became more and more unbearable. During this time Ken would go through a bad toe infection of gangrene and had to be hospitalized to have it amputated. He also had to have vascular surgery to help improve the circulation in the extremity the toe was infected in. Blood transfusions were needed, then after he arrived home, I had to give him his antibiotic therapy. Ken eventually recovered well from the surgery.

One day Ken approached me and told me about this experienced he'd just had. He told me he was in the bedroom smoking weed, then all of a sudden he was going through the house beating on things, then he went outside of our home and beat upon the fence. He would go on to tell me that he felt like God was talking to him and telling him things. He shared with me that he saw his whole life flash before him. He would go on to say that the voice would tell him that he was "the one." So there were times I would question him and try to understand what was going on with him, and what he meant by being "the one." I noticed he would become so angry and hostile. He just became so bizarre in his behavior and conversations. I didn't know what to think. He would reject the Bible more and more. As I would listen to him, he would say things contrary to the Word of God and against Jesus. He always wanted to talk about the word or religion, but it always turned him into a rage when I would quote the truth of the scriptures behind what he was saying. I was confused and frightened at the same time because I didn't know what had happened to him. It got to the point to where that's all he would talk about was "the experience." The Lord would later reveal to me that an angel of light spirit had taken over him (2

Cor. 11:14). And no marvel, for Satan himself, is transformed into an angel of light.

One time Ken wanted me to hear something. He began making the strangest sounds as if he was growling. Again, I was very frightened. As time went on, and the arguments and fights kept getting worse. I feared for mine and my children's safety. Going over into 2011, we had only been back together for one year, before I'd asked him to leave again. I filed a restraining order on him, hoping that would get him out the house. His lawyer would show up in court with him again, and the order was thrown out. He refused, so one day while he was at the dialysis clinic, I packed my kids and I some clothes and went and stayed with my folks for about three weeks and came back. Of course, nothing changed. More silent treatments, more distance, more anger, and insanity. I couldn't hardly believe what I was going through again.

After much contemplation, prayer and fasting for 21 days (first time, I'd done a straight liquid fast only). I'd gotten enough strength to pack up my entire house after being there eight years and left with my kids. We moved into an apartment. Ken eventually moved in with his family. The kids and I finally had some peace at our new place for a while. I would still allow them to visit with their father on the weekends. We only communicated concerning the kids, that was it. Later on, once I'd gotten settled, my financial situation was looking worse and worse. I tried to sell my house, and work something out with the mortgage company. I eventually had to file for bankruptcy and place the house and many other things under that. I couldn't imagine how much worse things could possibly get, and they did.

Chapter 11
PARADISE PARANOIA

Our apartment was so beautiful and peaceful. I loved going onto the balcony being able to talk to the Lord and read my bible. It would be so peaceful. The kids could swim and enjoyed their new schools. I continued in church and trying to do what the Lord was calling me to do. Towards the fall of 2012, the kids and I were attending a local church that we thought we could grow in a be there a while. While we were there, we met a family that we would eventually become close with, and I allowed them to move into our apartment with us. The husband and wife had just reconciled their marriage. Josie had just gotten full custody of her seven children. Delivered from a life of drugs and prostitution. After having to leave their place they were staying at that time, they were having difficulty getting stable, and. (Oh Lord, must I relive this?) Josie, her husband, and six of her children moved into a three-bedroom apartment with us. By this time, it was Jan. 2013, and I had to let my job go. The Lord had been pressing on me to stop working. Jan. 1, 2013, I contacted my manager at the time and told her that I was not coming back to work. The next thing I did, was fell on my knees and prayed to the Lord to give me the grace, strength, and peace to go through whatever I was about to go through.

My life went through some levels of changes again; I didn't think I was going to survive. Of course, everyone thought I was really crazy for quitting my job. In Matthew 5:19-20 we read "And he saith unto them, Follow me, and I will make you fishers of men. And they straightway left their nets, and followed him." The Lord had been dealing with my heart about this test of my faith that I would have to endure. He reminded me about the call He gave to the disciples. He reminded me about how He tested Abraham with Isaac, and how He provided for him. He would go on to confirm His will for me through other servants to make me know without a doubt this is what He was telling me to do. I had to go through it.

I really liked and grew to love Josie and her family. I believed them when they said after they got their income tax money that they would leave and find them somewhere to stay. I made it very clear to them, and out of concern for them that I did not want them trying to stay here with me to help pay bills because it was so expensive. Of course, they agreed. We were all going to church together and having prayer, trying to raise our families up in the admonition of the Lord. Everything seemed to be going alright for a while. When I could no longer work, one prayer I made unto the Lord, was not to let us go hungry.

My money eventually ran out, and none of us were working. Josie was getting a little over thousand dollars in food stamps each month(I know right), and she would sell at least 300 to 500 dollars worth each month, then try to skimp on the food. I loved to cook, so I would prepare big meals. That eventually became a problem. Josie began to feel as though the food was going too fast and would try make everybody live off of cereal and sandwiches every month. At this point, I began to question my own sanity about what I was allowing and what was taken place. They didn't have any transportation so I found myself going back and forth, at least 30 to 45 minute travel time every day taking her and her kids. I mean my gas light stayed on. It stayed on so much as we drove miles and miles back and forth around the city, until one day the Lord put a word on my heart, "how far can you go on empty?" Lord have mercy, I was on empty, not only the gas tank but at this point, I was literally drained and tired of everything and everybody. Empty of energy, empty of money, empty of peace, joy, you name it. I was so done.

The Lord was still faithful. He would allow people to bless us with money when we go out and pass out gospel tracts. The Lord opened a door for me to do some part-time teaching at a training school for nursing assistants. It worked out because I had to bring Josie to this place almost every day for her volunteer service in order to keep her welfare benefits. You know I was so grateful for this, wasn't near what I was used to bringing home as a nurse, but it definitely helped get us through. The Lord, would allow me to teach a student who was living a lesbian lifestyle. I was able to minister to her about God's love, and show her in the scriptures about what God says about this sin and how she could be delivered and set free from it.

I not only neglected myself for these people, but my children suffered greatly. Arguments, and attacks started to increase. Josie would finally go so far and accuse my daughter of trying to come on to her husband. What in the world have I allowed in my home and amongst my children? I would find out later that drug use still bound Josie. She was very abusive to her very passive husband. He was afraid to speak up for himself. This lady continued trying to accuse my daughter of things. She would take all of the knives from the kitchen drawer and hide them at night because she thought my daughter would harm someone. I wanted these people away from us so bad. It's like I had to wait until everything ran its course. I felt so horrible and ashamed. I believe I also allowed the madness to continue out of fear of being without. At least my kids and I were able to eat and keep a roof over our head, for now.

April 2013. "Man, they done put a eviction notice on the door!" "We got until May." Things began to get more and intense in the apartment as we started to think of what to do. Josie's plan was for us all to move into another apartment together. She and her husband had no ID, credit bad, no car, all of the income tax money gone, 5 thousand some dollars. Here I am, at one point I felt like I was at the mercy of these people. I was even considering going with them. During this 3 month period of living with Josie and her family, I became so alienated from my family. Only because of God's grace and mercy, only because I could still pray and cry out to Him, did I survive once more. May 2013 it was time to leave. Thank You Jesus! My children and I would be free from this situation.

I did not have money for storage for my belongings. At this point again, I didn't care. I was going to let them have it all. I believe this was the only reason Josie was able to sell enough food stamps to rent a moving truck for my furniture. My grandmother helped me get the storage unit and took care of the monthly payments. Packing up and leaving the apartment was so chaotic. My place of paradise had turned into a pit that I couldn't wait to escape. As we were leaving for the final time, I could sense that Josie was furious. "So where do you all want to go," I asked. "Just take us to the shelter," Josie responded. As calm as I could, I told her no, and that I couldn't just take them to the shelter and drop them off. Plus it was a Sunday, and the shelter was probably closed or was not going to take them in. I told Josie that I would just take them to her Aunt's house, who lived next door to the church we were attending. Josie immediately begins cussing me out, and yelling at me, calling me out my name in front of her husband and children. I remained very calm and said very little to her as I was driving.

Once we arrived at her Aunt's house, she continued cussing me out. I went inside the church, crying and upset. Josie followed me in the church, yelling and continued calling me names. I just sat there, and the Lord just kept me calm. By this point, nothing but devastation and relieved at the same time. One of the greatest lessons I learned going through this experience with Josie and her family was never to make decisions based your emotions when dealing with individuals with the kinds of issues they were facing. We must use wisdom, which is the Word of God and much prayer in order to know and discern how to help people. We must not have any hidden motives and plots going on either within ourselves, thinking "well, I'm going to get something out of this," and it end up backfiring. My initial intentions and motives were good and honest when I decided to help Josie and her family. But, again, I allowed my emotions and poor judgment to cause me to stumble in this situation. Josie's expertise in emotional manipulation and deception added more lighter fluid to this fire.

Chapter 12
FROM HURRICANE TO TORNADO

My kids and I had to move back into my folks home. The last place I wanted to be also. Strangely, I was relieved from one disaster to immediately go into another one. Of course, my folks were very angry, and couldn't understand why I wasn't working. It was like I was about to relive my childhood all over again with this man, but now with my own children. Lord, why? I hadn't taken all of my belongings out of my truck yet. My stepfather and I had gotten into it so badly. I got in the truck and drove to the corner store and was making a decision to just live out of my truck or go to a shelter. After praying and getting myself together, I believe it was that following day; I went to see if I could get us in a shelter. After filling out the paperwork and telling them my situation, the lady stated, "if we give you some place to stay, it will only be for two weeks." I pretty much said forget it after that. I was getting five-hundred and some dollars in food stamps. It was all I could help out with at the time. I just couldn't understand why the Lord would allow me to return here. Why? I cried and cried. So many arguments after arguments. Then I found myself in a constant battle trying to protect my kids from the emotional and verbal abuse. I didn't' feel like their child. I felt like a complete stranger. I thank God I continued going to prayer and church. I would go to the library almost daily to look for jobs. I had finally got an interview for a home health agency. It went really well. I was so excited. Days past no callback. I wondered what had happened. Later to find out, I didn't get hired, because my nursing license had expired. Lord have mercy!

During this time at my mother's house, the Lord had allowed me to take care of my cousin Niella. We were able to be a great strength for each during that time. She loaned me the money to get my nursing license back. After I was able to get my nursing license back, I reapplied to the same home health agency, got another interview, and they still didn't hire me. Okay Lord, what are You telling me. While I was applying for jobs and waiting, the Lord opened a door for me to work and earn $9 and something an hour taking care of Niella, who was bedridden. Lord, You tell me I have gone from six figures to $9 per hour. In Philippians 4:11-12, the Bible says, "Not that I speak in respect of want, for I have learned. In whatsoever state I am, therewith to be content. I know both how to be abased, and I know how to abound: everywhere and in all things I am instructed both to be full and to be hungry, both to abound and to suffer need."

The only way I was coming out, Jesus would have to deliver me again. But I was desperately trying to focus on God's purpose for this all, holding on to His promise, that all these things were working for my good because I love Him and I was called according to His purpose.

During my baths at night, I would sit in that tub for at least 1 to 2 hours, just resting and talking to God. It was so amazing.

It was as if God was hiding me and protecting me. I could be in there knowing He brought me to my folk's house, but didn't leave and drop me off like we do our kids at a time. But He stayed and was there with me the entire time. How glorious Jesus is!!! Father had to help me to realize that even though He had sent me to Babylon, He was still going to take good care of us. I had to fight with the weapons of my warfare and the whole armor of God, if I was coming out alive. Even more, knowing that He was on my side. I remember having a moment when I was literally having a conversation with the Lord about just taking me away out of this world. I had to stop the arguing back and fighting. Humble myself in this fire and trust God.

Chapter 13
NOBODY BUT GOD

The pressure and weight of everything began to get so overbearing. I just wanted out again. I suddenly began having a longing and desire to have my family back again. Yes, I was longing to be with my husband, my children all together again. So I began praying and talking to Father about it. He was dealing with my heart about Ken. This was the summer of 2013. Ken and I began talking again and having long midnight conversations like we teenagers again. I was really happy we were talking and bonding once more. At first, It was some hesitancy on Ken's part, but I knew my mind was made up about us reconciling and being a family again. Ken was living with his uncle at the time, so he had help with his living expenses. It was a relief for the kids and I to go over there and spend time with him away from my folks house. I was so happy again and being close to him. Ken was always the laid-back, quiet type until you got to know him. He had a great sense of humor and was a very gifted writer and poet. He loved to make music also.

"Why is his head so cool?" I would think to myself. But I didn't make much of it. As a dialysis patient, staying cold a lot was one of the side effects of treatment and due to chronic anemia. I just fell back into my role as his wife, trying to make him feel at rest and to trust me again. I tried so hard not to upset him. I wanted to make sure I was doing my part as a wife. I knew the Lord was with us and had a great plan. Our children were so excited and happy again. I was just so grateful that God was giving us another chance. It felt so good dating again and just hanging out and doing what couples do, and just anticipating being back in our own place again.

Praise God I had finally gotten a call for my new job. Back in dialysis, I really didn't want to go back into dialysis, but at this point again, a job is a job. Man, I was so broke. All these past days, weeks, and months not being able to afford much gas, the light staying on, and depending on others, my very first week of orientation, I run out of gas on the street. Lord have mercy! But the Lord gave me strength to keep pressing. I was so grateful to be working again, I refused to let that shake me. Things were beginning to look up. I was now able to pay some money back to my folks and help out with the bills. It felt so great working again and earning money. The Lord was moving swiftly. Four months after I began working , the Lord blessed us with our own place again in March 2014. I was able to pay my grandmother back and get my belongings out of storage. Thank You Lord Jesus! The kids and I settled in our new place beautifully. I had enough money to move in, buy my appliances and take care all needed expenses.

The kids were so happy, now we were just waiting for Ken to come home. Ken had made the decision to stay with his uncle until June of 2014. That's when the lease was up, which was only fair to continue his share of the expenses. Plus it gave the kids and I time to adjust, settle, and taking on major responsibilities again. The day finally arrived for us to pack up all of Ken's things and bring him home. We did just that! Once Ken got home, I knew it would take so much more adjusting and getting things in order with our family. Everyone had changed in so many ways. That summer of 2014, we drove all the way to Myrtle Beach, South Carolina. We had the best time. I loved it; the kids did too. Ken enjoyed himself too, but he was reserved as usual. We all were tired from the drive. We ate good food, amusement rides for the kids, and walked the strip. The beach and pool were so lovely. We spent four days in Myrtle Beach; then Ken decided that he wanted to drive all the way back to Memphis for eleven hours without my help. I was grateful he felt like it, and he had the strength too.

Chapter 14
HIS MERCY ENDURES FOREVER

"Hey, how are y'all doing?" I asked. I was finishing up my shift that Saturday afternoon, when I called to check on Ken and the kids. "They okay," Ken replied. "I'm not feeling good. I been nauseated and feeling like I got to throw up." Ken went on to tell me that he was having chest pains and that the pain started to go down his arm. He went on to tell me that he was feeling weak. I told him to go ahead and go to the emergency room and to call the ambulance. I let him know that I would be getting off soon, and would come up there to see him. He hung up the phone. I left work between 3:30 and 4:00 that afternoon. I went home to check on our children, and changed clothes. I made it to the emergency room where Ken was lying on a stretcher being waited on. I went and sat next to his side. I tried to keep the questions to a minimum, and he wasn't saying much. He did say the pain was still there. The nurse went on to share with me, that Ken's EKG was abnormal, and that his potassium was high. Being a nurse, I knew this was not good at all. "We are going to have to redraw the potassium level, and take him down for a cardiac catheterization, the E.R. nurse stated. We were also waiting for them to get Ken a room transfer. While waiting, I decided to go into the bathroom to take a few deep breaths and try to take in all that was going on. "We have room for him," the ER nurse stated. We finally made it to the room and got Ken settled in. He was feeling a little better after the morphine they gave him to help relieve the pain. Still not saying much. It was a few minutes to seven o'clock; I decided to get back to the house to rest and check on the kids. Ken was sitting up on the bed, and I just told him I would check on him later, and to let me know what they say. I left.

"Is this Mrs. Petty?" Yes, this is. "Mrs. Petty, we took Mr. Petty down for a cardiac cath, and things turned for the worst. We need for you to come to the hospital", the voice on the other end stated. This was close to midnight. I quickly said okay, and hung up the phone. When I arrived at the hospital, they told me that Ken "coded" on the table during the procedure. (a term used to describe when someone's heart has stopped, and needed resuscitation). They had transferred him to cardiac intensive care unit. Ken was attached to the ventilator (breathing machine), and a cardiac pump to keep his heart going in order to profuse his body. They also had him on medication to keep him sedated so that he could relax, and allow the machines to work for him. I remained at Ken's beside throughout the night until around 5 am that morning. Praying for him, trying to comfort and reassure him. I believed he could hear me. I was just calling on the name of Jesus, Jesus, Jesus! Lord have mercy! I felt how the Spirit of God was upholding me and walking me through this journey. I finally went home that early Sunday morning to contact Ken's family to let them know what was going on. Ken's father made it into town to be with us. We held on believing for the best outcome for Ken.

Later on that Sunday afternoon, the kids and I made it the hospital. They didn't have much to say; then tears finally came to their faces. Lord, please keep my children and don't allow this to destroy them, was my prayer. They became a little lighter in their spirits later on that evening. At one point with some quiet time with the Father, he spoke in my spirit, that this sickness was not unto death. I started rejoicing in my spirit. I went home and found where Father had given that word to Mary and Martha, concerning Lazarus's death. (John 11:4 When Jesus heard that, he said, This sickness is not unto death, but for the glory of God, that the Son of God might be glorified thereby.) Oh, Jesus how wonderful You are! He was with us every moment of the way in this situation. The kids and I decided to get back home to prepare for work and school the next day. I felt some reassurance in my spirit that Ken was going to be alright. Ken was resting, and things were quiet.

I got up the next morning and went to work. I was thinking to just go on in, trying to relieve my mind of some of the things that were going on, and if I needed to get to the hospital quickly, amazingly my job was literally right next door to the hospital. It was around 7 a.m. that morning. I received the phone call that Ken was not doing well, and that he was "coding" off and on. Meaning he was dying, and that they had to keep resuscitating him. I quickly left the job; this was September 1, 2014, Labor day. They were increasing the medications needed to keep his blood pressure and heart rate sustained normally. We continued to pray and pray as Ken continued to fight and fight. "Mam, do you want us to continue?" Yes please do whatever you can. The doctors and nurses were absolutely some soldiers that came to fight on this battlefield. I appreciate them so much how they were doing what they had been placed there to do. They were truly in this fight with us. I saw their tears, their passion, my God. I thank You forever.

"We are going to call it"! The machines turned off, the medications stopped, the room cleared. Just like that. Ken could finally be at rest now. No more, no more, this battle is over. I got closer to Ken, held his face and hollered. All I remembered saying was, "I prayed and I prayed for him." He was gone. We stayed there a while and waited until Ken's brother arrived. I went home later to get our kids to bring them to see their father. My mother also joined us.

What could I have done differently? Did I do enough? Why didn't I make him go to the doctor? Questions began to bombard my mind. Lord, I thought we would spend the rest of our lives together. Lord, I thought he was going to be alright when You said this sickness was not unto death. But Father kept me pressing in and meditating on that whole chapter about Lazarus and how He resurrected him. To go a bit deeper in why He came and the true and resurrected life He came to bring man, after the physical death, but life eternal with Him.

> Jesus said unto her, I am the resurrection, and the life: he that believeth in me, though he were dead, yet shall he live: And whosoever liveth and believeth in me shall never die. Believest thou this? I bless Your Holy Name Jesus forever! Mighty Deliverer You are.
>
> John 11:25-26

Chapter 15
TIL DEATH DO US PART

can't do this. I have never done this before. I don't want to make funeral arrangements. God had to pour out more grace and strength upon me to handle the next phase of this process. Something inside of me was just wanting to refuse to do it. About a month before Ken passed, God laid it on me to purchase a life insurance/burial policy for Ken. When I approached Ken about it. He became very upset with, and yes it turned into an argument. So I just left it alone with him, and went behind his back to try and get something in place. Well, after Ken had passed, and due to the timing of his death, and when the policy was initiated, it was not honored. I had to come up with the money to bury him. I was able to borrow $2500, family and friends gave approximately $1400, then I pawned my truck title for $2400. In all the funeral was $6100. I was able to find Ken a really nice gray suit with blue accessories. Even though Ken wasn't the suit-wearing kinda guy, he looked really nice in it. I thought about putting a hat on his head, since he wore them almost daily, but I didn't. It was one of the hardest things again, I would have to do. BUT GOD!! . Everyone began to step in and help me get things in place. His family, and my family, friends, co-workers, and Ken's caregivers at the dialysis clinic were very supportive to me and the kids. Even after I had the funeral paid for, people were still donating money for me and the kids.

September 13, 2014 we are here now to say our final good-byes. We marched in as the preacher read from Isaiah 40, one of my favorite chapters. Then we sat down to prepare for the service. Ken's cousin, Minister Rogers stood up in his place in the pulpit as he prepared to bring the word. Father confirmed His awesome Presence and Word miraculously in my life once more. Minister Rogers preached from John chapter 11, about Lazarus. The same word Father spoke to my spirit concerning Ken while he was in the hospital. I just looked up and threw my head back in amazement to our Great God, Lord and King. I hadn't seen, heard from, nor talk to Minister Rogers until that moment, that day of Ken's funeral. God is God! He is all powerful and all wonderful. He speaks to us through His Spirit and His Word. I was so blessed and joy came over my soul. I knew God had heard my cries and prayers, and Ken was with Him. Hallelujah! His mercy is from everlasting to everlasting. His mercy endures forever. I was so grateful Father had allowed Ken to come back home to us, before He took him to his eternal home. I was so grateful that God had allowed me to be at his bedside, praying and interceding and comforting him in his very last hours. I'm forever grateful that after we'd face and gone through together, we parted in love and peace. Ken departed this life in peace after so much he'd suffered. Some dreams not being fulfilled, many hurts, many disappointments. BUT GOD receives all the glory, because Ken received the greatest reward we all are praying to obtain, and that's to spend eternity with our heavenly Father and Creator God, forever and forever. Amen.

Chapter 16

SIN BROUGHT THE DELIVERER

Due to the stain of sin that entered into our world after God created man, we have had to live with the curses that rebellion, transgressions and iniquity brought upon us. Our Creator told us who He wanted us to be, but we chose the opposite of an identity created in His Image and likeness. We chose the corrupt and defiled image. The image that would contaminate and destroy our minds, bodies, souls, and spirits is the image of death and destruction. We chose to worship the creations instead of the Creator. The Lord knew this from the very beginning of the ages that Satan would be the god of this world that would cause Adam(man) to be separated from Him and removed from the Garden, removed from His Presence. So the Lord already had a most awesome, most glorious plan to bring us back to Himself. By His Love, By His Son, Our Lord, Our King Jesus the Christ, who would save us from our sins and reconcile us back unto Our Father, Our Creator. We thank Him forever and ever. Amen

And all things are of God, who hath reconciled us to himself by Jesus Christ, and hath given to us the ministry of reconciliation. (2 Cor. 5:18).

I am eternally grateful that the Lord Jesus Christ delivered me from a defile and corrupt identity manifested through sexual perversion, drug and alcohol abuse, adultery, fornication, greed, covetousness, and depression. The cleansing Word of God freed me and gave me my true identity in Christ. His Love, His mercy, His grace freed me. A testimony of the power of God's reconciliation unto us.

Chapter 17
KEN SPEAKS

HE BROUGHT ME BACK
By: Kendrick Mario "Petty the Poet"

I have been lost. I have worshipped idol gods that were false, I have overlooked Jesus Christ on the cross but,
He brought me back.

I have been attacked thrown off the right track—hating everyone that wasn't black, but,
He brought me back.

I left home, with satan I have roamed, couldn't differentiate right from wrong, but
He brought me back.

In the wilderness I was left alone, so many blessings have come and gone—dark places I have known, but
He brought me back.

Backslide is what I did—what was so small has gotten so big—took my sins, ran out and hid, but
He brought me back.

I have gone thru violence, sickness and fear. Silence sent me as sheep among wolves, while they were howling and growling, but He brought me back.

Dealing with worldly women and men—backstabbing friends—I felt like sacrificed meat thrown in the lion's den, but

HE BROUGHT ME BACK (CONTINUED)

He brought me back.

Not so close with my family, lack of communication have damaged me, negative thoughts use to manage me, but

He brought me back.

I went into an unfertile place, death staring me directly in my face, look back at all time that I had waste, but

He brought me back.

LIFE TO LEGACY, LLC

Let us bring your story to life! Life to Legacy offers the following publishing services: manuscript development, editing, transcription services, ghostwriting, cover design, copyright services, ISBN assignment, worldwide distribution, and eBooks.

Throughout the entire production process, you maintain control over your project. Even if you have no manuscript, we can ghostwrite your story for you from audio recordings or legible handwritten documents. Whether print-on-demand or trade publishing, we have publishing packages to meet your needs. We make the production and publishing processes easy for you.

We also specialize in family history books so that you can leave a written legacy for your children, grandchildren, and others. You put your story in our hands, and we'll bring it to literary life!

Please visit our website: www.Life2Legacy.com
Or call us at: 877-267-7477

www.ingramcontent.com/pod-product-compliance
Lightning Source LLC
LaVergne TN
LVHW011413080426
835511LV00005B/511